Into Perfect Spheres
Such Holes Are Pierced

Into Perfect Spheres
Such Holes Are Pierced

Catherine Barnett

Catherine Barnett

For Michael,

Who understands and
sings so beautifully —

— Catherine

June 2005 NYC

ALICE JAMES BOOKS
FARMINGTON, MAINE

10 9 8 7 6 5 4 3 2

Alice James Books are published by Alice James Poetry Cooperative, Inc.,
an affiliate of the University of Maine at Farmington.

Alice James Books
238 Main Street
Farmington, ME 04938

www.alicejamesbooks.org

Library of Congress Cataloging-in-Publication Data
Barnett, Catherine, 1960-
  Into perfect spheres such holes are pierced / Catherine Barnett.
    p. cm.
  ISBN 1-882295-45-5
1. Elegiac poetry, American.   2. Family—Poetry.
3. Death—Poetry.   4. Grief—Poetry.   5. Girls—Poetry. I. Title.
PS3602.A7757158 2004
  8113.6—DC22

2003024341

Alice James Book gratefully acknowledges support from the University of Maine at
Farmington and the National Endowment for the Arts. 🐝

Art Credit: Jean-Luc Mylayne. "No. 63 Janvier Février 1987," 1987. C-print, 73 x 73 inches
(185.4 x 185.4 cm). Courtesy Barbara Gladstone.

Acknowledgments

Grateful acknowledgment is made to the editors of the following publications, in which these poems, sometimes in slightly different versions, first appeared: *Barrow Street:* frontispiece (as "Untitled"); *GSU Review:* "Meditation on Falling"; *The Hat:* "Home," "Pitch and Black Lift," "Story"; *Interim:* "The Disbelieving," "Part to Stand for Whole," "Site, IV"; *The Iowa Review:* "Child Learning to Write," "Journal"; *The Massachusetts Review:* "Refusal"; *Pleiades:* "Ritual," "The Return."

My gratitude to my teachers and friends who advised this book in manuscript and who sustain me as a writer. It is a privilege also to thank, for years of friendship and guidance, Ellen Bryant Voigt, Ruth Danon, Miranda Field, Alexandra Enders, Susan Karwoska, Eleanor Wilner, Tom Thompson, Carl Dennis, Joan Moore, Chris Edgar, Andrew Boynton, Kathleen Peirce, and Claudia Rankine. For the ground they hold beneath my feet, I thank my sisters, my brother, my parents, my son.

Contents

III

C minus A and B equals—
Tree with no branch equals—

What grief looks like:
A knife rusted in the side of a goat.

No, no.
A coin falling in water

And the fish dart for it.

I

The Return

For a long time there were no signs though we looked
    wildly for them.
Of course there were lawyers, they came to the house,
lawyers might have been a sign—

And the birds in the park, circling us—

And the DNA, which Aristotle
would have called the fourth kind of recognition,
not what we invent (oh the girls come to us in dreams)
or what we remember, on waking, but—

Someone resembling me has come:
No one resembles me but them:
Therefore they have come.

From the Fence Around the School

hang white ribbons,
letters to the dead
written down the silk.

When the rains come
it makes no sense
but the ink doesn't bleed,

the crêpe stays so flush
you'd think the fence in bloom
as you might think my sister untying

the ribbons to bring home
was only cutting flowers
from a black vine.

Aubade

Irregular song, irregular heartbeat,
anaphora's

stutter that neither
warns nor comforts:

I thought it was a man's voice
all this time, calling for help.

I thought it was a man
calling scared from the ditch.

Hopeless barking it was, a dog trapped
somewhere, and lonely—

then suddenly quiet.
Someone must have hitched her collar up,

stitched her mouth down,
or shot her dead—

how else break such pitch.

Transcript

1.
You can read one version in the newspaper
and another in the courts
and a third in my sister's face,
in my sister's sisters' faces,
in my mother's face—

in the candles burned down to their jars—

2.
How can there be no whole bodies?
You never told me—

We hid the newspapers, the tv, the radio,
the record, the report, the story, the letter, the transcript,
the black box, the irrefutable, the true, the wrong,
the doorbell, the singing, the sky.

3.
And their voices gone, too—

4.
Not just quiet,
not just sleeping past the hour of waking up,
past the sun rising, the alarm, the schedule of rushing,
the falling of leaves, the freezing river, the thawing, the last thawing
and then the later and later setting of the sun
until it's almost day all night
and still the girls don't wake
but my sister keeps waiting
and there's enough for her to do until they do wake,
she can tidy up, dust,
cut the crust off every piece of bread
and turn the lust for them
into some impossible having,
some impossession
shutting down her ears and mouth
so she takes nothing in but grows larger and larger as if
into her body she could take and hold them

not just the story of them

5.
not just the story of them
before the jackscrew and rust slipped
and the plane came to fly upside down
and the pilots, jesus, flew it upside down
and said, in private, only
here we go, here we go.

Nits

It was their father's weekend to take them
and he packed their bags without thinking
last anything. *They can't go,* my sister said.
They've still got lice.
But they did go and while they were gone
she boiled their brushes until like rice the nits
rose to the surface, vanished, then
reappeared as flecks of pale ash in the soapy water.

With a slotted spoon she lifted the brushes
from their bath and left them bristle-down to dry.
Around each one she twisted the glittery bands
her girls loved to braid through their hair and carried them
all fine and clean upstairs to the beds she'd vacuumed and remade
with fresh flannel sheets for the last day of January
when her girls would be coming back to her
and find nothing changed but all the nits gone
and the dust gone and even the smells of their own
bodies washed away.

Site

The dirty sand everyone said was beautiful
wasn't—it was dirty, or oily,
something turning it to hardness.
It was ugly when we were told
beautiful, shattering when it was
supposed to make us whole, cold
when it should have been warm
and all of us dressed in wrong clothes
because everything was wrong.

We walked the beach early,
lay down in the sand, and tried to sleep
there in the dune hardly a dune it was so low,
but away from the wind—

The locals told us not much ever
washes up on the beach.

How cold it got down by the water.
The water was cold.
The windsurfer wore a wet suit and sailed
back and forth like the birds.

Living Room Altar

Except for the shirt pulled from the ocean,
except for her hands, which keep folding the shirt,
except for her body, which once held their bodies,

my sister wants everything back now—

If there were a god who could out of empty shells
carried by waves to shore
make amends—

If the ocean saved in a jar
could keep from turning to salt—

She's hearing things:

bird calling to bird,
cat outside the door,
thorn of the blackberry against the trellis.

Ritual

In his bath my son looks half-
drowned,
lying so still,

his hair a scarf of weed,
his eyes closed,
and only the water breathing.

He practices
in his porcelain bed
his resting,

rehearsing
until the water takes cold
and he shivers a little against it.

After Trying to Calculate
the Weight of a Six-Year-Old

Went to the field and picked blueberries for a long while,
boxes and boxes of them—

It was quiet, no cannons firing
to scare the birds.
(No birds there.)

~

Bought a watch with a face so tiny
you can hardly see it

~

And we're watching it and in it at the same time

~

this hole she wants to spend all her money to dig—

~

Too expensive, I tell my son when he longs
for the yellow fireman's jacket,
the yellow boots,
the black plastic ax with the black plastic handle.
Not now—

~

They say the plane disappeared into the ocean—
they don't say anything about the ocean,

how the ocean was changed

~

My sister says maybe this happened
even before it happened because everything
happens at once.

~

My son watches us make fire.
He wants black leather wings to fly with.

~

For example, if you keep halving the distance
from sky to water
you should never get to water.

~

eighty-three passengers,
five crew,
negative three g's,
250 miles an hour,
700 fathoms down

~

quiet field—

Duration

I bought a game of clocks to teach my son time
and when we started to play I thought

how cruel—

how in a field of dirt the paleontologist after years of searching
finds the beautiful body,

the fossil—

how the priest dips green leaves into water—

how resurrection—

how my son brings broken sticks to me—

how into the sky how my sister stares—

Site, II

We were all *she's* there—
sister, sister, sister, mother, friend, friend—
and by then we knew.
We sat on the floor in the mortuary looking as if for beauty
at a plate of jewelry and a room full of urns.
One urn pale wood,
one urn with two cloisonné cranes,
one urn blue steel with four bolts underneath.
My sister took a small brass cube from the velvet plate
and two hollow stars and a screw-top heart
she's to fill with ash and hang from chains
around her neck. What was she thinking?
Who could pour ash into such tiny shapes?
And whose ash?
For one child we had a penny bag,
for the other not a thing.

As by Giving or Letting Go

How to tend to their belongings—
Mend them?

Spend them?
Send them to us who still have children

though we try not to speak of them,
frightened as we are.

Lent to my son and me:
four cartoon plates, a box for lost teeth,

and a homemade board game
with a sack of markers and dice.

For a child of six and a child of eight
it must have been ecstasy to count so high!

What my sister can't give away
let her break, remake,

take out of the closet the red velvet dress
her eldest wore one Thanksgiving in high fever

when we pressed our hands to her forehead
to cool her, fool the child to sleep.

II

The Disbelieving

We all saw how beautiful she looked
those first six months when she walked a thousand miles—
over the University Bridge

and under it
and into and out of the Arboretum
and up the hill to the sundial we circled every day

while the days got longer
and my sister more beautiful,
her red hair turning gray, a slow

turning, as if some force were braiding out the red,
and we looked at her
through veils—

veil of gray hair,
veil of hands over face,
veil of disbelief we all shared then.

The night after we picked up the ashes
she drew the brass urn into bed with her
and in the morning pulled back the blankets—

I've fallen asleep next to her
and I've awakened next to her
and every morning is every time

the mother lifting the sheet to see her child
sleeping and dreaming only the bed is empty
and the mother strips the blankets

and strips the sheets
down to the mattress made of stone.

Into Perfect Spheres Such Holes Are Pierced

We unstrung necklaces into two glass bowls
and passed them round to the mourners.
The beads were onyx, agate, quartz, all manner

of stone. Everyone was to take two
and at the end of the service
put one back in my sister's hands.

What could she do but collect
the round weights all night?
She has not restrung them,

not wanting to be finished yet with death.

Refusal

The god of footprints accepts no prayers, he's
a cheap and sweaty god who must have lost his mind.
It's dark with my back turned but what else is there to do?
Fine, fine, yes, yes, she's surviving,
don't ask me again.
We only hummed with the rabbi
but my son heard us sing *die, die, die, die.*
He's just turned four and on his face
there's a strange pleasure when he says *died,*
as if he'd seen a door in a mountain—
but there's only my sister's house
and the string of profanity
I tie to the empty chairs we drag behind us.
And every window is a curse,
something to break that shatters.
The two birds we saw on our usual walk
were blue and gold, they flew
too close to the ground.
Upstairs the girls' room does not change
and I sleep there now, when I come to visit.
I prefer the high bed, but I can't say why.

The Return, II

My brother thinks it's best to distract my sister,
not ask her about longing and its dirty tricks,
its flirty tricks, her girls

oh, hiding under the sheet waiting to be found,
digging ditches in the dirt,
blowing out the candles—

He holds her up, his arm over her shoulders
so she won't see the eyelashes they leave there,
for luck, like she taught them,
for making wishes that can't be spoken aloud

but I know he hears them,
as she does,
asking the same thing again—

come with us—   come with us—

Site, III

There was so much wind as we walked
we had to bend forward
like the whitecaps in the harbor
that was no harbor just a piece of ocean
where the ocean was a grave with no flowers
even after we threw the wrong-colored roses
down to the waves.

And there was still the walk back,
back out of all this now too much for us—
the birds diving into the high hard water
then coming up for air some distance away, how far away
or how long it took we don't know.

One of us measured longitude,
then latitude, and we saw that what looked like two
was really one island, a true shore,
the one we couldn't get to on account of the wind.

Portrait

Like a branch hanging down and blackened:
there's no crutch left in me,
no plank or board
just wood turning soft all over
but at the hitch of stubborn blossom
where I've fastened to my sister
in whom radiance is grief,
shiny and polished,
pitch and sap to her roots.

Still Life with No End

Every day in her studio my mother
sets out to paint the large picture, to fix
the order of the planets and their circling,
to find which universe is ice and which fire,
which the limit and which the spreading forth.

When the paint dries she scrapes it flat.
Begins again, upside down.
And the cold thing stares back.
Bold stare. Look of the harrowed.
Downstroke at the brows,
erasure of the rising mark.

Two Girls, White Sky

At first to soothe their mother
they were the brush in her hand,

then the hair on her head,
the lash around her eye,

and then when she slept the bowed
line of her eyes they tried to stitch closed

against waking,
against the sky that took—or is—

their place, that is every morning
the wide hard open

of their mother's gaze, gaze they want
to get closer to, inside,

inside her glazed cathedral eyes
unfamiliar now as bloodshot marble that nothing penetrates

as nothing penetrates
the satiny voids in a dead bird's head—

such abandoned beauty.

What the Naked Eye Looks for
but Cannot Find

Why ask her to wake?
So she can look into the sky at what?
The stars keep her company but niggardly so.
She watches them as they fall, pointing out
the tiny invisibles of black
where stars have been named for her girls
who can't be seen with the naked eye
though we all pretend to follow the map she draws
into the cloak of holes.

While My Sister Sleeps

I straighten up best I can the closet under the stairs
where her daughter's silver coat
has pooled onto the floor,
a dusty moon slipped off its hanger.

Hung back up
it makes a cold light—

O furious disorder giving way to order!
The girls' things—

two wishbones saved for breaking,
shells, bells, whistles, dolls,
a hall of games
tidied into a bright spine,
empty ingots of bone against bone
that ring out from the narrow house—

Reverse it—

Site, IV

At the bottom of the ocean—
even there—
the bones are picked clean.
I suppose this must be common,
this relentless cleaning,
and the tiny sequin
tossed into the bin of dirty water
and our eyes gouged out with looking.
Oh.
Child.
When did the child die?
And how white are the whale's bones.
There, down there.
How did you wait for me this morning.
Oh sequin.
Eye.
Our hearts evolved
from our throats—

Journal

26 january, flying west

yesterday a year ago was the last time she spoke to her children

five-days-before-they-died

isn't it homeopathic, the ocean now?
dilutions of her first daughter diluted
into not-penance-but-ocean-now

the could-have-beens!
the sparkling house

28 january, my sister's house, Seattle

so what are we to make of the whole disappearing?

the girls' books and notes and keychains are lit with dust
and dust is just skin so I wonder—
are they here in the dust

in the paper this morning
a partial list of what-was-found
bandana-slash-camera-slash-jeans

in two days they're burying all unidentified remains
in a common grave

my mother keeps trying to paint

the bird outside the window doesn't take off
but gets caught in the branches
and the sky's all tangled, too, reluctant to get bright

even claire's hair is getting light

29 january, *beach house, morning on Vashon Island*

what but the water being high
and it being colder than usual, earlier than usual
and my sister waking in the dark
and there being no clock so what time it is she only wonders
not moving because not wanting to move
though outside the water is all movement
and glass gets washed up on the island
reminding us how even heavy things
tend toward shore while my sister in her bed
waits for it to get light
so it will get dark again
and everything in between is impossible
and so is the getting-to-sleep
and the waking-up and even to lie by her side
is almost impossible
my body like eyes reading some incomprehensible text

who asks *is she better now?*
who's cleared the shore of every piece of washed glass,
restored the scattered glass all softened
and battered by the waves
to its former state—a vase on a windowsill one spring day
with yellow flowers and fresh water
and a penny for good luck and to keep the flowers from wilting?

there is no other light, she says, it's all dark here

the same front page says 15,000 people killed in an earthquake,
they keep trying to dig them out—

is it better to have someone to blame?

cold this morning—

31 january, *small gathering in my mother's home, Seattle*

my niece wore a t-shirt with a yellow smiley face,
the shirt my sister claims from the coroner's catalogue

everything unclaimed got buried together
and it fit in one coffin

we lit eighty-eight candles,
they weren't supposed to drip
but the colored wax spilled off the mantelpiece
right down to the floor

sometimes I try to convince claire the girls aren't dead
the plane didn't go down

you're sick and lossened my friend told me in a dream
she said it mean but it was the truth

lossened sounds like *lozenge,*
something to suck on, a tiny flange to shunt
under the wobbly tongue

there was candlelight on my mother's face
as she shaped the wax drippings into tiny rafts,
held wax to the flame and taught my son what to do

how to make islands of wax,
bodies of wax, branches—

in that light she looked like a candle,
pain lit up, as in church

what's unfinished is what we love—
the ceiling at St. Mark's Cathedral
and its raw beams

we don't finish, we leave the door unlocked

Theology

1.

When God dies the children in the family skit
carry him out of the yard as practiced:
stick under his knees, extras holding the branch
that for the moment doesn't break only bends so low
the child's hair drags in the dirt.

2.

In the newspaper a priest admits tidiness is not
part of God's plan,
that what plan there is might mean nothing—

3.

Everyone dies, the schoolgirl says to her teacher,
and what could the teacher say?

4.

The empty can on the lawn catches the rain,
half in conservation,
half wanting to know how much has fallen.

5.

The rations of illumination and grief—

6.
In the landscape there's no one
though that's all our eyes seek.

Idiot eyes,
caught in longing.

7.
If theft is a kind of love,
in this way God could be said to love.

Evening in the Garden

At the edge of the field where rare species
had overgrown a corner of the school playground,
some kind souls built a garden.

They made a spiral path with sea glass
the children separated by color,
one boy sorting each kind of green

from every other. I looked hard for something
to like because I thought my sister,
leaning against the marble wall where her daughters' names

were carved, might want me to find beauty there.
I saw her youngest daughter was named first
and I thought oh!

I never noticed there were two в's in her name,
that must be why the marble looks so strange—
alliteration—

or the lettering, or the stone itself,
or the ledge against which
lay the small shiny whisk broom

I admired, too,
until my sister began sweeping the path,
until my son took the broom from her

39

and began sweeping things not meant to be swept,
the edge of the flower beds raised up in a row,
the benches, all made out of the same enormous stone.

Meditation on Falling

Sometimes to outwit love
I think I should throw my son
from my arms, or from the window,
or from the bridge where we watch the sun
light up the underbelly of cloud.
Hold me better, he says.

On falling, a shirt
fills with air—like a kite!
A hat flutters, a shoe
might be mistaken for a bird,
a necklace unfasten hook from eye
until the sky

in borrowed clothes
rises through the body
as in rage, or rapture.

Part to Stand for Whole

Expert at her puzzles, my sister
is working in broken mirror,

a thousand pieces laid out on her table.
Who looks down

fades in one fragment, is gone
in another.

When I come to visit
she leaves the best pieces out for me.

It's part of our game—her praise,
my pretending, my pretending to find them myself,

to make the broken faces swimming back at us
come whole.

Vashon Island, Washington

1.

Out on the beach we hardly noticed the shells,
we wanted sea glass, one piece for every day of the year
because we can't do what we did last year,
we can't have another birthday party
with only other people's children
now so many have gone and gotten older,
taller, almost taller than my sister, and scared of her—

they're a funhouse mirror she's looking into—

2.

We know time's passing
because the ferries still shuttle back and forth.
One morning we saw what looked like an island
being pulled right across the Sound,
and sailing up so far ahead it seemed impossible
it could be fastened to anything,
the small tugboat.

3.

And the fat wet pyre of stripped trees laid horizontally
on the glassy morning water moves so slowly
it's as if it won't get anywhere but where it already is.

4.
Every day the tide comes right up to the porch.
My sister watches it come in, go out, and once we found
a seal washed up on shore.
I remember it had no head and I think I know why—
those tugboats with their long tow lines
like a knife in water. We didn't speak about the seal
and I half forgot because I have the luxury of forgetting.

For my sister, one day is really no worse than any other,
longing stretched so tight it's a wire dragged through water—

Ninth Birthday
—for Coriander

On rainy days like this how empty the park is.
We push the seeds a quarter inch down,
two per inch. They're round and black,
like water beads on glass,
and they like cool weather,
guaranteed to bolt slowly when they do.
Were we to bite into one,
it would at first taste bitter,
then like wine or soap burn our tongues.
We stand under the apple trees,
the only gardeners out on a day like this,
unseasonably cold for late August,
and the harder it rains the better we feel.

As If by Fastening

Out of their old clothes—

out of hems out of stitches out of pleats out of collars
out of velvet out of rayon out of lace out of ribbon
out of yarn out of wool out of bows out of laces tied in knots
out of shoes lined up at the door out of mud out of dust
out of air out of the closet's empty stare—

what can my sister make?

Sail, veil, ladder, quilt.
Flag to raise,
rope to lower:
exit, escape, something to drape out the window
and climb the fathoms down,
down the rope of clothes left behind,
clothes not packed for the trip.

Book of Lies

1.

My sister's smile before disappearing is an uneven
tear in the blank sheet of her face.

In the book of lies it says there are eighteen kinds of smiles—
it says look for lies in the opening and closing of the mouth.

2.

We gave out no stones at the service this year
but before disappearing the torn day got shorter,
the grief archive gave out its last ration

and we all stashed our troubles on my sister's lowest shelf.
It was something I once loved to do,
putting like things with like.

Home

1.

At night with the lights off my son asks, *where are you,*
which way are you facing?

I'm facing you, I say.

2.

What is that small triangle
opening at his throat,
where his hand likes to rest?

3.

We have a vase of broken sticks,
and I find them beautiful
but he tapes them back up.

I don't want a broken thing, he says.

4.

When he's in pain
I can't fix it.
His lips hurt so I touch
the edge of his mouth.

5.

It's not usually this dark, he says.

III

Body of Water, Body of Glass

1.

The black swivel chairs in my parents' house
don't face the view, the Sound with its ferryboats
and hang-gliders, Mount Rainier and the path of jets.

They face the interior, filled with the breakable:
the garden window, the cocktail table,
the vases, bottles, jars my mother glazes and fires
until the glass itself takes on color.

2.

Empty now, lying on the floor by the fireplace,
glazed so many times it's gone opaque,
the five-gallon jug used to balance on our cooler.
Sad planet! How vast it had seemed—

When we were children it was a shimmery
see-through blue we lined up to drink from,
holding down the spigot until our cups ran over.

3.

Without flowers, without water, without breaking,
centered on the back sill, glass almost touching glass,
the tallest of my mother's vases opens wide at the top,
pulls in at the waist, a wash of violent color:

no hourglass, no life study, just a figure in the void
—silhouette, witness, portrait, ghost—
trying to let light pass through.

Family Reunion

My father scolded us all for refusing his liquor.
He kept buying tequila, and steak for the grill,
until finally we joined him, making margaritas,
cutting the fat off the bone.

When he saw how we drank, my sister
shredding the black labels into her glass
while his remaining grandchildren
dragged their thin bunk bed mattresses

first out to the lawn to play
then farther up the field to sleep next to her,
I think it was then he changed,
something in him died. He's gentler now,

quiet, losing weight though every night
he eats the same ice cream he always ate
only now he's not drinking,
he doesn't fall asleep with the spoon in his hand,

he waits for my mother to come lie down with him.

Still Life with Departure

I watch my mother pack, tell her
leave something behind.
She's wearing the black shoes I lent her,

and they fit her so much better than they ever fit me
she wants to keep them,
says she could walk forever in them.

For a long time she thought if she made one circle,
and circled that circle, she could keep us safe.
For a while it was true,

until the circles we were got filled with other circles,
water inside water, beginning inside end,
mouths inside each mouth and all calling.

Still Life with Paper and Thread

Open-mouthed, propped against the bureau,
the holes in their chests covered by blue velveteen,
my two CPR figures never say anything.
I'm supposed to practice rescuing them,

the big one and the little one,
but it's my son who plays with them, he's
the one who's read the instructions,
who folds the thin admonitions into airplanes

he hangs from the ceiling with black thread.
When the wind comes in from the river
the papers above his bed sway back and forth.

Child Learning to Write

1.

At church he practices writing *no*
then copies some words from the prayer book.

2.

When I dress him in the morning
I pull on his shirt, pointing out the hole for his head,
for his hands, for his entire body.

What does vanish mean? he asks.

3.

He keeps the ink between the lines
as he jags the pen up and down, sad
because he doesn't know what he's writing.

4.
Out of *grief*—
ire,
fig,
fire.

5.

Painted like a bird, labeled *shrike* across its wings,
the shiny toy breaks.
We tape it back up, matching the lines

the torn letters make.

Love is like this—

Poor shrike, hurling its body against the ground.

Pitch and Black Lift

Where my father's hip was rejoined
his leg lost an inch or two.

His right shoe is a ladder,
a shadow under him,

a hearse of black rubber he can't escape.
He stands before the shoemaker

in his old bare feet
shaking off sadness,

a boy shaking pebbles out of his shoe.

Dinosaur Park

I'm cutting you open, my son said,
stroking his friend's chest with a stick.

Do it harder, the friend said,
and my son, nodding yes, scratch-blessed

the boy's flesh then lay down
and pulled his own shirt so high

his whole ribcage showed.
The boys heard me call.

Go away, my son said to me.
Look away.

I was any scarecrow, any hawk,
watching as all birds watch the world's

machinery.
I stared at the fiberglass dinosaurs

until I could see their chicken-wire veins.
I stared at the fence, the chain,

the solder in the chain.
To keep from staring I stared

into the band of trees hovering
above the familiar territory—

above the boys, the blacktop,
above the row of benches where I sat carrying on

with the other loud birds.

Scratch Harvest

This spring hail hit the apples
and the tiny marks became divots.

Into the stew pot more apples,
still in their skin and pocked.

Smooth black seeds
keep rising to the surface.

Outside, the trees are oblivious
to the disorder of their bodies,

the divots in their offspring
bear them no shame.

It's all the same to them,
same sweet flesh,

same irregular songs sung
by the mockingbird as by the wind,

and all beautiful, the same song
sung by footsteps

as by shears radiant against
the black branches.

Story

He's in the park again, shaking leaves from trees,
pulling buds from branches,
turning over rock and stone

until he gets to the high stone wall
where the dirt's caught
in the petals of the early daffodils,

where the mica in the dirt shines so much
he thinks he's found what he's been looking for—
aphids for the beetle kept in a jar.

He saves the dirt, the stone, the flower,
and the jar fills up with flecks
so small and shiny they could almost be

the necessary angels.
Who else will feed the dead like he does?
When his mother finds out, she'll bury the jar—

Just before the beetle died, it showed the boy
how it could walk in circles, walk upside down.

Memento Mori

Why trust this world—
this one here with just the two peaches
and the watch leaning on its side
and the flashlight showing like an x-ray my bones
and the shale split into pieces like it never belonged together
and the drum of the boy's hand against his body
and the coals still warm from last night's fire
and no birds in the birdhouse
and the arms of the trees stretching upwards
and the match held, the tiny flame crawling,
and the boat inside my body filled with useless debris,
the boat upending and turning face down,
and the words carved into my wedding ring faded
and the wanting what can't be had
and the tick on my son's neck that won't let go
and the worms inside his body, open field his body is,
and the door that gives and the door that takes away
and last night's fortune, *nothing is beyond all repair*,
and the mother in me all tied up in a fine white line,
line we burn the edges of to keep from unraveling,
and the tiny narrative for tying knots
and the child I thought I might once again carry
and grief, the sheen we bring to wood
when with repetitive gestures we polish the raw thing.

Broken Clock

At the hour of astronomical twilight
when all stars are visible to the searching eye

you say it's morning,
your truant hands shaken and blue,

ungoverned by the weight on the weightless line
that keeps your time.

How you lie and cry
your prodigal hours,

that ditchy cluck starting up again
pretending happiness! joy!

Son with Older Boys

Half-men, half-dressed, they play baseball with him
on a summer field and the more they hit at it
the more the plastic ball, catbird of their games,
breaks—

half of it gone now. And the light half gone, too.
Indisputable. Already he's four,

soon five. I'm forty,
soon fifty, and it's evening now, time to stop playing
and it's hopeless but beautiful
how they wrap the ball in layers of masking tape
until it looks like a half moon
falling into and out of their game,
which lasts a little longer now for their troubles.

River

Because here, this far east, this far away,
there's no Pacific, no sister, no clock set to the real time,
I go down to the Hudson whenever I can.

More broken than usual,
all churned up and shaky, the river this morning
makes no progress to speak of, nothing much floats by
but a few red leaves caught on the rocks.
The water takes water into itself,

as if by emptying it could be filled,
or filled, emptied—

and I see it's not all gray—

where the water rises up there's shadow,
where the buoy is chained there's chain and rust
and a still white bird turns sideways
like another face.

Notes

"The Return": The italicized lines are from S. H. Butcher's translation of Aristotle's *Poetics*, in which Aristotle, to distinguish between four different types of recognition in tragedy, quotes Aeschylus' *Choephori*.

"Duration": In 1990, the amateur paleontologist Sue Hendrickson discovered the most complete *Tyrannosaurus rex* ever found. The dinosaur was buried for 67 million years in a riverbed near Faith, South Dakota.

"Refusal": The phrase "door in a mountain" is from Jean Valentine.

"Site, III": "Back out of all this now too much for us" is the opening line of Robert Frost's poem "Directive."

ALICE JAMES BOOKS has been publishing exclusively poetry since 1973. One of the few presses in the country that is run collectively, the cooperative selects manuscripts for publication through both regional and national annual competitions. New regional authors become active members of the cooperative, participating in the editorial decisions of the press. The press, which historically has placed an emphasis on publishing women poets, was named for Alice James, sister of William and Henry, whose fine journal and gift for writing went unrecognized within her lifetime.

Typeset and Designed by Dede Cummings
Printed by Thomson-Shore